SALAMANDERS AND NEWTS AS A NEW PE

CONTENTS

Inside front cover: marbled salamander, *Ambystoma opacum.* Inside back cover: longtail salamander, *Eurycea longicauda.* Photos by R.T. Zappalorti.

t.f.h.

© **1994 T.F.H. Publications, Inc.**

Distributed in the UNITED STATES to the Pet Trade by T.F.H. Publications, Inc., One T.F.H. Plaza, Neptune City, NJ 07753; distributed in the UNITED STATES to the Bookstore and Library Trade by National Book Network, Inc. 4720 Boston Way, Lanham MD 20706; in CANADA to the Pet Trade by H & L Pet Supplies Inc., 27 Kingston Crescent, Kitchener, Ontario N2B 2T6; Rolf C. Hagen Ltd., 3225 Sartelon Street, Montreal 382 Quebec; in CANADA to the Book Trade by Macmillan of Canada (A Division of Canada Publishing Corporation), 164 Commander Boulevard, Agincourt, Ontario M1S 3C7; in ENGLAND by T.F.H. Publications, PO Box 15, Waterlooville PO7 6BQ; in AUSTRALIA AND THE SOUTH PACIFIC by T.F.H. (Australia), Pty. Ltd., Box 149, Brookvale 2100 N.S.W., Australia; in NEW ZEALAND by Brooklands Aquarium Ltd. 5 McGiven Drive, New Plymouth, RD1 New Zealand; in Japan by T.F.H. Publications, Japan—Jiro Tsuda, 10-12-3 Ohjidai, Sakura, Chiba 285, Japan; in SOUTH AFRICA by Multipet Pty. Ltd., P.O. Box 35347, Northway, 4065, South Africa. Published by T.F.H. Publications, Inc.
MANUFACTURED IN THE UNITED STATES OF AMERICA BY T.F.H. PUBLICATIONS, INC.

Natural History

This book is dedicated to a group of people who have an interest in the tailed amphibians, the salamanders and the newts, and who wish to begin with one of these fascinating creatures as a new pet. The salamanders and newts are closely related to the frogs and the toads, but are sufficiently unique to warrant a volume of their own. The following chapters hopefully will guide the prospective salamander enthusiast into the many years of pleasure these fascinating creatures can surely provide.

Salamanders and newts belong to the order Caudata (which literally means "tailed") of the class Amphibia, which they share with the frogs and toads and the little known caecilians (mainly tropical limbless, burrowing creatures with a superficial resemblance to large earthworms).

Zoologists list over 4000 living amphibian species, the vast majority of which are frogs or toads. The tailed amphibians, the salamanders and the newts, comprise about 360 species or less than 10% of the total number of amphibian species. However, the complexity of the species, particularly some of those from Central and South America and from Southeast Asia, makes it highly probable that further new species will be described in the foreseeable future.

CLASSIFICATION

Zoological and botanical classification are necessities. When you consider the enormous numbers of animals and plants on earth, a system of categorizing is obviously essential. Over the ages a number of scientists attempted to develop systems of classification, but it was not until the 18th century that a "sensible" system arose. This was developed by Karl von Linne (1707-1778), a Swedish botanist, who made a list of all animals and plants known to him at the time in a work called *Systema Naturae*. In the work, each species was given a double Latin name, the generic and specific names.

As an example of the double name or binomial system of nomenclature, the mudpuppy

Necturus alabamensis, otherwise known as the Alabama waterdog, has no subspecies and thus is only given a binomial Latin name. Photo by R. D. Bartlett.

(a large aquatic salamander) of North America is given the scientific name *Necturus maculosus*, in which the first name is the generic name, the second being the specific. There are other species in the genus (*Necturus alabamensis, Necturus beyeri, Necturus lewisi, Necturus punctatus*), and all of these show similarities of structure that warrant them being placed in the same genus.

Species normally do not interbreed with each other. When on rare occasions they do (hybridization), infertile hybrids are usually the result.

BIOLOGY OF SALAMANDERS AND NEWTS

The life history of a salamander is, in general, less familiar to the average person than the life history of a frog. For some reason or other, the frog seems to be a much more popular subject for school biology lessons than the newt. However, if we are to keep our pet salamanders and newts in optimum conditions it is essential that we know something about their life cycles and behavior, especially if we intend to breed them.

A typical salamander has a soft moist skin, an elongate body, and a well-developed tail often as long as or longer than the body. Superficially, the shape resembles that of a lizard, for which the salamander is often mistaken. Closer examination of a salamander, however, will reveal no scales, no claws, and no external ear openings as possessed by the reptile. Most salamanders and their larvae are carnivorous (though the sirens may be partially herbivorous). The smaller species feed on insects, tiny crustaceans, worms, snails, etc., while some of the larger ones will take in addition any small vertebrates they can

overpower, including fishes, frogs, and other salamanders; a few will take carrion.

Most salamanders are nocturnal and very secretive in their habits; in fact, the average person is unlikely ever to see a salamander unless he goes looking for them in the right places. Unlike the frogs, to which salamanders are fairly closely related, salamanders are largely voiceless (there are a few exceptions that let out a sort of protest "squeak" when handled or attacked by a predator). Depending on the species, salamanders may be totally terrestrial, totally aquatic, or semiaquatic; several species typically are found in trees in the American tropics.

A great variety of breeding behavior is exhibited by the various species, ranging from simple meet-and-mate tactics to elaborate courtship rituals with well-developed sexual differences (the latter is particularly applicable to newts of the genus *Triturus*). In almost all cases fertilization is internal, but accomplished without copulation. The male deposits a gelatinous, pyramidal structure, the spermatophore, on the substrate. The spermatophore is capped by a capsule containing sperm. The whole object or at least the cap is retrieved by a receptive female with her cloacal lips, often as the male leads her over it during a courtship "walk." The

The mountain dusky salamander, *Desmognathus ochrophaeus*, shown here with a clutch of eggs, is more terrestrial than most dusky salamanders and usually breeds in the cooler months of the active season. Photo by R. T. Zappalorti.

spermatophore dissolves in the female's body but the sperm are stored for later use. When the eggs are laid (often weeks later), they are fertilized by the stored sperm.

The larvae of water-breeding species start feeding upon tiny aquatic animals within hours of hatching. Unlike all but the youngest tadpoles of frogs, the larvae have conspicuous, feathery external gills on either side of the head. The front limbs develop before the rear (the rear develop first in frogs).

Housing

Anyone intending to keep salamanders or newts must plan the accommodations required well in advance; it is not good policy to obtain the animals first and then start worrying about housing them. In most cases it is best to keep each species in a separate cage, not only so that differences in habitat or habits can be catered for, but because some species are unable to withstand the temperament and/or the body secretions of others! In addition, some species will not only eat other species almost as large as themselves, they may even eat their own brothers and sisters!

A cage in which small living animals are kept is called an aquarium, a terrarium, or an aquaterrarium. The first is used for keeping totally aquatic species, the second for terrestrial (land-dwelling) species, and the third for partly terrestrial (amphibious) species. By far the greatest number of amphibians falls into the last category as most require water in which to breed. In addition to knowing whether your chosen species is aquatic, terrestrial, or partly terrestrial, you should know something about its habits and native habitat so you can provide as near natural conditions as possible.

THE AQUARIUM

An aquarium tank can be used as an aquarium, a terrarium, or an aquaterrarium, but in this section we are dealing with an aquarium for totally aquatic species (axolotls or amphiumas, for example) where no land area is required. There are many kinds of aquarium tanks available on the market, from the somewhat old-fashioned steel-framed glass tanks to clear plastic and the common all-glass. All-glass tanks are by far the most satisfactory and decorative, at least for display tanks; other kinds can be used for breeding, rearing, quarantine, etc.

The dimensions of the tank will depend on the number and size of the animals you wish to keep, but it is wise to use no less than a tank 60 cm long by 30 cm wide by 30 cm deep (2 ft x 1 ft x 1 ft). Such a size would be suitable for a pair of axolotls. Remember that a tank full of water is very weighty; in the size mentioned above the water alone will weigh 54 kg (approximately 120 lbs), and to this we have to add the weight of the tank itself plus substrate and decorations (gravel and rocks are even heavier than water). Thus we have to ensure that the base and stand on which the tank is kept are very sturdily constructed and preferably reinforced with angle iron.

For display purposes it is good to create an environment in the tank that is as natural-looking as possible. Try and picture the sort of environment in which your chosen species lives in the wild. We must use compromises in many cases—river mud, for example, should be substituted with gravel—for obvious reasons. When setting up an aquascape for salamanders or newts, you can obtain many interesting tips from books about tropical or coldwater fishkeeping. Here it will suffice to say that a layer of washed aquarium gravel about 5 cm (2 in) deep at the front, sloping up to 7.5 cm (3 in) at the rear (deeper for larger tanks) should be placed on the floor of the tank.

For decorative purposes, you can use a few non-toxic rocks or river pebbles (granite, slate, etc., but limestone should be avoided) placed to form caves, valleys, and terraces. Pieces of treated bog wood can also be used to good effect. If you are keeping small aquatic newts and larvae, water plants may be cultivated in the substrate, but the continual grubbing actions of some of the larger species may make this a waste of time. The best method is to use only robust plants that are allowed to develop a stable root system before the animals are introduced.

THE AQUATERRARIUM

Most salamander species require an aquaterrarium with various ratios of land to water depending on the species being kept, although in most cases roughly half land and half water will be adequate. An aquaterrarium is also ideal for breeding many species and is especially useful for rearing larvae to their terrestrial stage.

An all-glass aquarium tank can be used, with the addition of a glass partition about 15 cm (6 in) high attached with silicone cement across the bottom of the tank to make a waterproof barrier between the land and the water. The water area can be given a 2.5 cm (1 in) layer of fine grade aquarium gravel, thus giving a water depth of 12.5 cm (5 in). To provide easy exit from

A species like this eastern tiger salamander, *Ambystoma tigrinum tigrinum*, is best kept in an aquaterrarium with a few plants. Photo by R. T. Zappalorti.

9

the water, a gradient of rocks and pebbles can be placed up the side of the glass partition.

The land area is half-filled with stones and coarse gravel to provide drainage (ideally a drainage hole should be incorporated into the floor of this area), then a mixture of sterilized garden loam, peat,

and recreation." The pots can be sunk into the substrate or concealed behind rocks, bark, etc. If possible, use plants that are compatible with the conditions in the tank and, for authenticity, try and get plant species that come from the same part of the world as your salamanders.

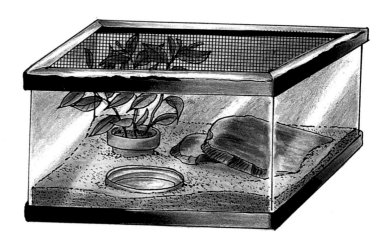

This is a terrarium that has both good and bad points for salamander keeping. The rocks, the plant, and the water bowl are all perfectly acceptable, but the sandy substrate is no good, and the top is too "open," thus doing nothing to help retain humidity. Drawing by John R. Quinn.

and coarse sand (commercial potting mix is ideal) is placed on top to fill in the area and to slope up and away from the water. A slab of turf or pieces of moss may be placed over this, coupled with mossy bark or stones to form hiding places. Plants are preferably left in their pots so they can be changed easily. It often is difficult to get plants to fare well in a terrarium, so keep two sets of plants in rotation so one can be given regular periods of "rest

THE TERRARIUM

The terrarium is a container constructed for species that are totally or almost totally terrestrial and which do not require large volumes of water in which to breed (plethodontid salamanders, for example). A glass-fronted wooden cage may be used, but as you are likely to require a high humidity it is usually best to have an all-glass tank or a mixture of glass and acrylic sheeting (plexiglass). The advantages of plexiglass are that

it can be easily drilled and shaped and is ideal for sliding ventilation panels to be affixed on one or more sides. The main panels should be of high quality glass, so that crystal-clear viewing is possible.

A suitable size for a group of perhaps six plethodontids would be 75 x 50 x 50 cm tall (30 x 20 x 20 in). A layer of clean gravel is placed in the base and can be covered with slabs of living moss (which may have to be changed regularly). A piece of rotting log is placed in the center of the substrate and can be decorated with living epiphytic plants. In addition, or alternatively, a potted creeping plant can be used to provide extra interest and cover for the salamanders.

One of the most satisfactory means of heating a terrarium is to use the aquarium heaters manufactured for tropical fish tanks. There are many makes, sizes, and strengths available from pet shops, but most consist of a heating element and a thermostat housed in a toughened glass tube sealed with a waterproof stopper through which the power cable passes. The thermostat can be set so that a constant temperature is achieved. To heat the water in an aquarium, the

One of the more underrated salamander genera is *Bolitoglossa*, known in some places as the "club-footed" salamanders. They are very attractive, and require a warm, humid, neo-tropical type of setup. Photo of *Bolitoglossa platydactyla* by Robert S. Simmons.

The axolotl, *Ambystoma mexicanum*, one of the most commonly kept salamander species, never develops beyond its larval stage and thus is totally aquatic. Photo by P. W. Scott.

heater is simply placed in the water and the thermostat correctly adjusted. In an aquaterrarium, the heater will increase the temperature of the air space as well as improve humidity. In a dry terrarium, the heater can be placed in a concealed container of water (topped off daily), where it will act as both a heater and a humidifier.

At one time an ordinary domestic light bulb was the standard form of heating for a small terrarium. Indeed, there is certainly nothing wrong with using these lamps; they are cheap and come in various sizes. By experimenting with the wattages, you will come up with the optimum temperature. One disadvantage is that species requiring warmth at night will be inflicted with "continuous daylight" unless you use a blue or red bulb. If you require the bulb to light the terrarium during the day, the answer is to have two bulbs, a clear one for daytime and a colored one for nighttime. The colored bulb should be of a smaller wattage so that at the same time you can create a cooler nighttime temperature.

Heat lamps should be used with caution as the amount of radiant heat they emit can be dangerous to both plants and animals. If used, the lamp should be preferably placed outside the tank and directed through the gauze or mesh in the lid. The correct temperature can be achieved by experimentally moving the lamp up or down. For most salamander and newt species, heat lamps are totally unnecessary and actually

dangerous. Hot lights cause thin-skinned salamanders to desiccate in a matter of minutes, with death following quickly thereafter.

Other forms of heating that may be considered include heating cables and heating pads. They are used by horticulturists to provide "bottom heat" for their plants. The cables can be passed through the substrate, while pads are placed beneath.

As salamanders and newts are ectothermic (cold-blooded), they adjust their body temperatures by moving through a range of external temperatures. (This applies mainly to terrestrial species or species during their terrestrial

Many salamander species spend virtually all of their time underground, and therefore are probably not very desirable to the keeper. Shown here is the mole salamander, *Ambystoma talpoideum*, a notorious burrower. Photo by R. T. Zappalorti.

13

animals will then be able to select a spot to rest where they feel most comfortable.

In most areas there is a temperature drop at night; this may be as little as 3°C (5.4°F) in low-level equatorial areas, but can be as much as 20°C (36°F) or more in montane, continental, or temperate climates. Most species will benefit from a compromise reduction in temperature of 5-10°C (about 8-15°F) at night. This can be achieved by simply switching off the heater each evening and switching it on again each morning. The prevailing room temperature in the average house will be satisfactory for most salamanders and newts at night, except during the coldest winter nights.

Seasonal variations in temperature must also be taken into consideration. The breeding cycles of most species are affected one way or another by seasonal climatic changes, so reduced winter temperatures are important for many species.

LIGHTING

Most species of salamander and newt are nocturnal and/or crepuscular (active at dusk and dawn) and very secretive. Even those that are active during the day tend to move about in areas of heavy shade. This, however, does not mean that lighting is unimportant to our amphibians.

Certain salamander and newt species need artificial heating. Learn about the particular needs of those that you are keeping before purchasing any equipment. Photo courtesy by Zoo Med.

stage and not so much to aquatic species, where constant temperatures are more the norm.) Each species has its own preferred optimum temperature. To allow captive amphibians to select their own preferred temperatures in the confines of the terrarium, it is advisable to have a range of temperatures, a gradient. This is easily achieved by supplying heat at only one end of the terrarium. The warmest area will then be near the heater, and the temperature will drop gradually with distance from the heat source. The

As with most animals, the biorhythms of salamanders and newts are affected by photoperiod (daily duration of light). Many species rest during the day and know that it is time to become active as the sun goes down. Outside the tropics, seasonal changes of photoperiod are also a great influence on many species. The breeding cycles of temperate species are triggered by a combination of increasing periods of daylight and a gradual rise in temperature.

Successful breeding of your amphibians will only occur when you try and reproduce the dark/light cycle of their native habitat. If more than one species must be kept in the same terrarium, try and choose species that come from similar habitats and climatic areas. It is best to use artificial lighting in indoor terraria, as natural sunlight entering through glass will soon produce lethal temperatures unless the greatest of care is taken.

If your terrarium plants are to flourish, it is essential that the artificial light source you use is of the highest quality. Ongoing experiments with broad-spectrum (artificial daylight) light sources have produced some excellent systems. Horticultural lamps and fluorescent tubes that emit a quality of light ideal for plant

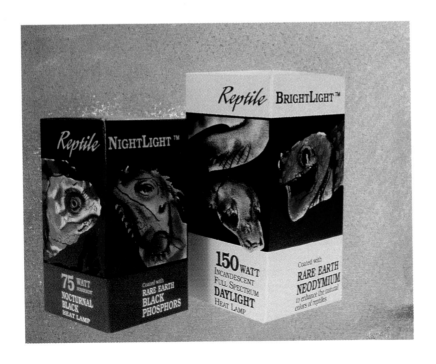

Special lights are not usually necessary with salamanders and newts, but having one can be very benificial to your reptiles. Photo courtesy of Energy Savers Unlimited, Inc.

growth are now available. The lamps come in all sorts of sizes, shapes, and wattages, and you will be able to find something suitable for every type of terrarium. Fluorescent tubes can be mounted on brackets and placed behind fine wire mesh (to protect the inmates) in the aquarium lid. Lamps that

VENTILATION AND HUMIDITY

Humidity and ventilation are closely tied to each other. If you have high humidity without ventilation, then the air in the terrarium will soon become foul, molds will develop on the substrate, bacteria will flourish, and there is a good

Although a bit on the flamboyant side, the terrarium depicted in this drawing is an aquaterrarium that could adequately house many salamander species.

tend to emit a great deal of heat should be placed outside the terrarium and directed through a gauze or mesh screen, or not used at all. Remember that salamanders are very subject to desiccation and do not respond well to either light or heat as a general rule.

chance your animals will get sick. Conversely, if you have too much ventilation and not enough humidity, the air will dry out very quickly, posing another danger to your moist-skinned amphibians.

Good ventilation will prevent a build-up of foul, organism-laden air and remove excess carbon dioxide, while adequate humidity will ensure that your amphibians flourish. The terrarium should have ventilation grills both in the sides as low as possible and in the lid. This will allow all of the air in the container to be exchanged constantly. If you use a heater, the convection currents created will speed up ventilation. An aerator in the water part of the aquaterrarium will not only provide additional ventilation, it will help maintain high humidity. Humidity can also be increased by regular (at least twice a day) mist spraying. Living plants will themselves help to keep the humidity high, as well as contribute to keeping the air fresh.

FILTRATION

The habits of aquatic and semiaquatic salamanders and newts mean that they are rather messy and will soon pollute the water in an aquarium or aquaterrarium. This means that the water will have to be changed rather frequently or you will have to install a filter. As it is not advisable to disturb your animals too frequently, it is better to use a filter.

The simplest type of filter is known as a box filter and is operated by an air pump. It usually consists of a plastic box filled loosely with a filter medium such as nylon wool. It

When setting up a filter, don't use just any carbon. This type from Living World is very reliable.

works on the principle that rising air bubbles create a current in the water. The air line (usually with a small air stone at the end) is placed at the bottom of the tube in the center of the filter. The rising air bubbles will create a current up the tube, and replacement water will flow through the filter medium, where suspended materials are removed. The filter medium is fairly easy to change at regular intervals. Such a filter is quite adequate for small volumes of water, especially if at weekly intervals part of the water is

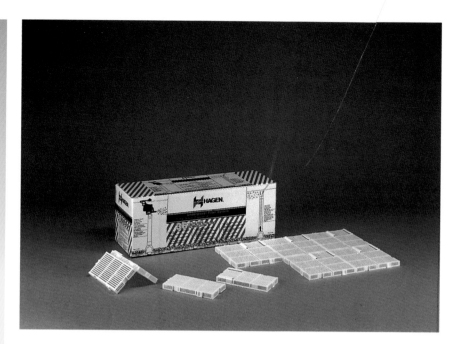

changed. For example, remove ten cupfuls and replace with a similar amount of clean, dechlorinated water at the proper temperature. Use of a filter provides much less disturbance than having to completely replace all of the water every few days.

For larger volumes of water it is best to use a power filter. There are many commercial types manufactured primarily for fish-keepers. They consist of a relatively large pump that removes water from the tank, forces it through a filter chamber, then returns it to the tank. For more details of such filters, consult your pet shop.

Foods and Feeding

In order to keep in prime condition, all animals require a balanced diet that contains the basic nutrients—proteins, carbohydrates, fats, vitamins, and minerals—in a ratio suitable for the animal in question. Different animals acquire their balanced diet in different ways, but salamanders and newts are almost totally carnivorous (with the exception of the sirens and the larvae of some species that may be partially herbivorous), feeding on a variety of invertebrates or, in the case of some of the larger species,

small vertebrates. It is the variety of food items consumed that ensures that the salamander gets all its requirements. Additionally, if herbivorous creatures are consumed by salamanders, the latter will receive a possibly beneficial amount of vegetable material in the diet in an indirect manner.

One of the major problems of salamander keeping can be a difficulty in obtaining an adequate supply and variety of food items in the correct sizes. Many salamanders will take only live foods, and it is the movement of the creatures that actually provokes a feeding response. Aquatic species may also rely on the senses of touch and smell, which explains why they will take carrion in the wild or strips of meat in captivity. There are a number of commercially raised invertebrates that can be purchased. You can also start your own cultures of various food items, which will save you money as well as provide you with a ready supply of food at all times.

COLLECTING LIVE FOODS

Perhaps the most satisfactory way of providing a variety of invertebrates for your amphibians is to collect items from the wild. Not only will this relieve the "boredom" that can arise from a monotonous supply of cultured foodstuffs, it will most certainly introduce additional beneficial nutrients to the diet of your salamanders.

The most productive method of collecting a variety of terrestrial insects and spiders is to "sweep" through herbage with a canvas-reinforced sweep-net. The mouth of the net is simply swept through the foliage of trees, shrubs, and tall grass, and the resulting catch is placed in glass or plastic containers for transport home. During the warmer months of the year, such sweepings will provide you with a great variety of beetles, bugs, caterpillars, grasshoppers, spiders, and so

You can also find a variety of invertebrates by turning over logs and rocks and other ground debris, where you will be sure to capture beetles, earthworms, pillbugs, slugs, and snails. Many small flies and beetles congregate in flower heads; these are very suitable for small salamander species and newly metamorphosed youngsters. They can be collected with a

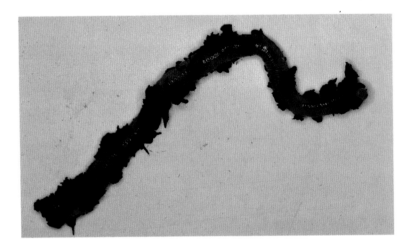

Earthworms are happily accepted by many herptiles, salamanders included. They are indeed a superb meal and play a very important role in the natural food chain. Photo by Michael Gilroy.

on. The collected insects should be graded into suitable sizes. These various invertebrates will be eagerly taken by your salamanders. It is best not to introduce too many insects at a time into the terrarium. Allow one lot to be devoured before adding the next or you will let escapees into the house or the insects will drown in the water and spoil.

"pooter" or slurp gun, which is a glass or plastic bottle with a cork through which two glass or rigid plastic tubes are passed. One tube, the mouthpiece, is bent over at right angles and passes just through the cork; the other tube is straight but ends near the bottom of the bottle. Over its outer end is placed a piece of flexible rubber tubing. The end of this tubing is placed near the insect to be collected and it is captured by sucking sharply on the mouthpiece. The insect will be drawn through the glass tube into the bottle. A piece of cotton wadding placed in the mouthpiece or a bit of fine mesh glued over it will prevent you from accidentally inhaling any insects.

A good food source for very small terrestrial salamanders is aphids (commonly called greenflies or blackflies). These congregate in large numbers on the growing tips of many plants (especially cultivated ones!). It is a simple matter to cut off a tip complete with its ration of aphids and place it in the terrarium.

Ants and termites can often be collected in large numbers. Though the ants are usually rejected by most salamander species (due to the formic acid taste), there are a few species that take good numbers of ants. Termites are taken eagerly by most species and are a particularly nutritious item. If you have access to termite nests, you can simply chip a piece of the mound or wood away at regular intervals, placing it, complete with the termites, in the terrarium. The nest will be quickly repaired by the termites left behind, leaving you with an almost continuous food supply.

Water-dwelling salamanders and carnivorous larvae require aquatic live foods. Various freshwater crustaceans, ranging from the tiny copepods and daphnia to the relatively large freshwater shrimps and crayfish can be netted or found by turning over rocks near the edges of streams, creeks, etc. The larvae of many flying insects (mosquitoes, mayflies, etc.) are aquatic and are also excellent food. When collecting aquatic live foods, be careful

Daphnia, although not often commercially available, are a good salamander food. If you look closely, you can see the eggs in the upper area of this specimen. Photo by Engasser.

not to introduce predatory types such as dragonfly nymphs or water beetle larvae which will make short work of some of your salamanders.

CULTURED LIVE FOODS

For various reasons, it is not always possible to provide your salamanders with collected live foods all the time. Maybe you are short of time for collecting (especially if you live in the city and would have to travel out into the country) or there may be very little live food about in the winter months of cooler areas. In such cases it is wise to have a standby supply of cultured live foods. Today there are many suppliers of various live foods. If you don't want to go to the trouble of breeding your own mealworms or crickets, for example, you can simply purchase a regular small supply of the insects. Some producers are glad to supply insects regularly by mail order. However, many hobbyists choose to culture their own live food, after having purchased the initial stock. The following is a brief guide to the

The mealworm beetle, shown below, is a nutritionally complete meal, but in its larval stage, shown above, it is not. Photos by Michael Gilroy.

more usual types of cultured live food.

Mealworms

The larvae of the flour beetle *Tenebrio molitor* are probably the most well-known and oldest commercially produced live food for pet animals. They may be purchased from dealers in any quantity and are relatively easy to cultivate. Allow a few of the mealworms to pupate and metamorphose into adult beetles (these are blackish brown and about 8 mm (0.3 in) long. The adult beetles are placed in a container with a close-fitting but ventilated (with gauze or fine wire mesh) lid, along with a 5-cm (2-in) layer of food mixture (bran and crushed oats are ideal). Place a piece of burlap over the food mixture

and put a couple of pieces of carrot, potato, or apple on top to provide moisture. The beetles will soon mate and lay eggs in the food mixture. It takes about seven days for the eggs to hatch into tiny mealworms. These develop to full size in about 15 weeks. By starting a new culture each month, a regular supply of mealworms of all sizes will be available. For the best results, cultures should be kept at temperatures of 25-30°C (77-86°F).

Crickets

In recent years cultured crickets have become a very popular live food for many insectivorous pets. They are easy to breed and very nutritious for your salamanders. There are several species available, but the most commonly encountered are domestic species of the genera *Gryllus* (usually blackish) and *Acheta* (often tan). Cricket cultures can be obtained from many pet shops. They come in various sizes from 3 to 25 mm (0.12 to 1 in), depending on what stage of the life cycle they are in. This means that there is a size to suit most salamanders.

Crickets are quite easy to breed in a ventilated plastic box kept at a temperature of about 25°C (77°F). Feed the crickets on a mixture of bran and

crushed oats, plus a little green food or raw root vegetable. A dish containing a piece of water-soaked cotton wool will double as a drinking fountain and a medium in which the insects can lay their eggs. The eggs will hatch in about 20 days, and the young can be reared to various sizes.

Flies

There are literally thousands of fly species, and most of these are ideal food for salamanders and newts. Fruitflies (*Drosophila*) have long been used as experimental insects in genetics laboratories. Due to the speed with which they reproduce, these little flies, about 3 mm (0.12 in) in length, have been found to be ideal for genetics experiments, and their breeding has been taken to a fine art. Even "wingless" (vestigial winged) specimens are bred in large numbers. These are very useful for feeding to small salamanders as you do not have the problem of flies escaping to all corners of the house. Fruitfly cultures and instructions on how to proliferate them may be obtained from some pet shops

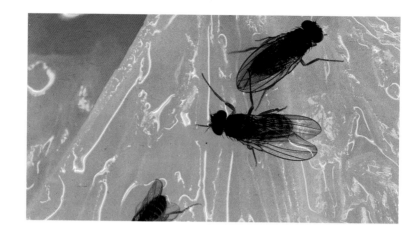

A colony of tiny fruitflies. Photo by Michael Gilroy.

or by mail order. Quantities of wild fruitflies also can be collected if you place a box of banana skins or some rotten fruit in a remote corner of the garden. During the warmer parts of the year, this will be teeming with fruitflies in no time at all. They can simply be collected with a fine-mesh net.

Houseflies (*Musca*) and lesser houseflies (*Fannia*) are suitable for small to medium-sized salamanders, while the larger greenbottles (*Lucilia*) and bluebottles (*Calliphora*) are suitable for your larger pets. Most of these can be caught in a flytrap in the summer.

Earthworms

Earthworms can be purchased from bait suppliers or can be collected in the garden or elsewhere. They are excellent food for larger salamanders and can be chopped into pieces for smaller ones. As pieces of earthworm continue to wriggle for some time after being chopped, they are accepted readily by many species. You can ensure a regular supply of earthworms by placing a pile of wet, dead leaves in a shady corner and covering it with a piece of sacking. If you spray the sacking with water regularly, earthworms will soon congregate among the decaying leaves, from where you can collect them at regular intervals. If one supply becomes exhausted, you can start again in another spot.

Tubifex

These are small aquatic worms that can be purchased from pet shops. They are a nutritious food and especially suitable for small aquatic salamanders, newts, and advanced larvae. Be sure the worms are clean and red in color, not gray. Dead or

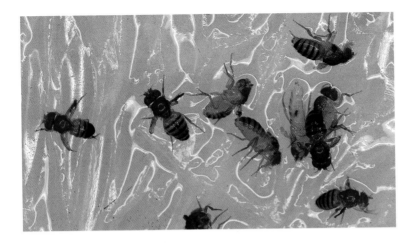

dirty tubifex worms can cause health problems or even death.

Whiteworms

These tiny worms can be purchased as cultures complete with instructions. They are a useful food for newly metamorphosed newts and for very small salamander species.

FOOD SUPPLEMENTS

In general, salamanders that receive a wide selection of live foods are unlikely to suffer mineral or vitamin deficiencies. However, where a variety of insects is in short supply (such as during the winter when we have to make do with cultured foods such as mealworms or crickets over long periods), it is advisable to give a vitamin and mineral supplement perhaps two or three times per week. Suitable vitamin and mineral preparations may be obtained in fluid, powder, or tablet form from pet shops. Powders are most suitable for vitamins as they can be dusted directly onto the live food. The insects are placed in a small container and powder is dusted over them. A gentle shake will ensure each insect has a film of powder over its surface; the insects are then given to your pets in the normal manner.

NONLIVING FOODS

Axolotls and other aquatic salamanders will take strips of meat or fish, and some will even take trout pellets or other manufactured foods. Do not feed fatty meat, but provide meat that is as lean as possible; the same goes for fish. Never feed more than the amphibians can eat at one time. A little every so often is better than too much at once, as the food will soon pollute the water.

Reproduction of Salamanders and Newts

Each individual species has its own unique breeding habits. The habits of those species included in this book will be briefly described later. Here we will take a more detailed look at a somewhat typical life cycle, followed by a brief general summary on the captive breeding of salamanders and newts.

LIFE CYCLE OF THE AXOLOTL

We know more about the life cycle of the axolotl, *Ambystoma mexicanum*, than perhaps any other species of salamander. This is because over the years the axolotl has been almost domesticated. Not only is it one of the most common of all "pet" amphibians, it has long been a popular item for biological research and education. It is the only salamander that may be legally kept as a pet in Australia (where it is commonly referred to as the "Mexican walking fish") and is, in fact, the only caudate legally present in that country outside zoos or research establishments.

The first Europeans to see live axolotls were probably the Spanish conquistadors who arrived in Mexico in the 16th century. The axolotl was said to be partially sacred to the original natives of the Lakes Xochimilcho and Chalco areas (near the present Mexico City) but it still appeared on the menu at certain times of the year. Wild axolotls may still be found in those same lakes today (assuming you can find an unpolluted area capable of sustaining life), but they now hold protected status.

In spite of its relative familiarity, the axolotl is an interesting amphibian that deserves a place in the collection of the salamander keeper. It is especially valuable to the beginner, being relatively easy to keep, feed, and breed. Another plus is that all available specimens are captive-bred, so there is no depletion of wild populations.

A sexually mature axolotl can reach a length of 25 cm (10

The axolotl, *Ambystoma mexicanum*, is probably the most commonly bred salamander in the world. However, it is remarkably rare in the wild, and will probably exist exclusively in captivity very soon. Photo by P. W. Scott.

in), though the average is more likely to be in the region of 20 cm (8 in). The "normally" colored axolotl, like its wild counterpart, is dark sooty brown with even darker brown to black spots and blotches. The underside is somewhat lighter. Captive stocks have produced a number of color mutations, including albinos, goldens, and pieds, the latter probably being the most attractive. The axolotl has a broad, shovel-like snout and a flattened head with a wide mouth. Its small, lidless eyes are wide-spaced but oriented toward the top of the head. The short but robust limbs are spaced well apart on the sturdy body, which sports a number of vertical (costal) grooves along the flanks. There are four fingers and five toes respectively on the fore- and hind-limbs (the normal number of almost all salamanders and frogs). A low crest starts just behind the head and runs along the vertebral column into the laterally flattened tail where it becomes wider. The crest also continues along the underside of the tail, which is used by the animal to swim and steer. The limbs are not used for swimming but may assist in braking and steering. They are mostly used for walking about on the substrate. The axolotl's most prominent feature is the pair of three-lobed feathery gills that project up to 2 cm (0.8 in) on either side of the head. These are deep reddish brown in normal specimens but bright crimson in albinos.

In the wild state axolotls are not known to metamorphose into terrestrial forms, but they can be persuaded to change into typical adult salamanders in captivity. Metamorphosed specimens become dark gray with yellow spots; the tail becomes round in section and the skin becomes smoother. This can be accomplished by gradually reducing the water depth over a period of several months. Once the water is about 2 cm (0.8 in) deep, the animals will be forced to start taking atmospheric oxygen. The process can also be halted at any stage almost up to full metamorphosis by again increasing the water depth and allowing the partially absorbed gills to redevelop. However, once the gills have been completely absorbed, the process is irreversible and the salamander would drown if forcibly kept below water.

The process of metamorphosis is evidently influenced by the amount of thyroxine produced by the thyroid gland. If injected with a small quantity, or immersed in a solution of this hormone, axolotls will develop into terrestrial forms. The introduction of minute quantities of iodine into the water in which axolotls are kept has been found to promote the production of thyroxine by the salamanders, also resulting in complete metamorphosis. The process of remaining as a larva and being able to reproduce in that state is known as neoteny, while

Habitat destruction and human development have led the axolotl to its endangered status. It is only found in the lakes of Mexico City and many experts believe it may already be extinct. Photo of a female by P. W. Scott.

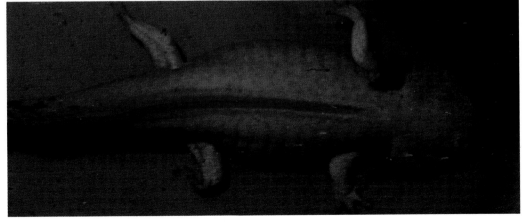

such reproduction itself is known as pedogenesis.

Another outstanding property of the axolotl (shared with many other salamanders) is its ability to regenerate limbs or gill filaments that have been lost accidentally or to predators (often other, larger axolotls). A new appendage, usually perfect in every detail, will grow within a few weeks to replace the missing one.

Axolotls can be housed in simple aquaria, no more than four specimens to a tank of 60 x 30 cm (2 ft x 1 ft). Depth should be somewhere between 20 and 30 cm (8 to 12 in). Clean aquarium gravel and a few pebbles for decoration may be placed on the substrate. The tank should be equipped with an aerator and a filter. Supplementary heating is unnecessary as axolotls will fare well at room temperatures and can tolerate a range of temperatures, though they seem to thrive best at 17-20°C (63-68°F).

Wild axolotls will eat almost any living creature they can overpower. In captivity they will take lean raw meat, which they seem to find by a combination of smell and touch. This, however, does not constitute a balanced diet and should only be a supplement to various live foods, such as earthworms, slugs, snails, mealworms, crickets, etc. Do not over-feed and allow uneaten food to remain in the tank, as you will be asking for trouble (fouling, smells, pollution, and ultimate death of your axolotls). In the absence of live foods over a period, it is wise to work a good quality vitamin and mineral powder into the lean meat. See what your pet shop has to offer.

Axolotls breed in the wintertime (usually February) in Mexico, when melting snows from surrounding mountains temporarily reduce temperatures in the lakes. In captivity this phenomenon can be simulated by adding ice cubes to the axolotl tank, thus subjecting the amphibians to thermal shock. This may be done at any time of the year, but best successes take place during the months from December to mid-July. Adult axolotls of both sexes are

Look closely. Do you see the tiny tubifex worms? These are a fine food source for axolotls. Photo by P. W. Scott.

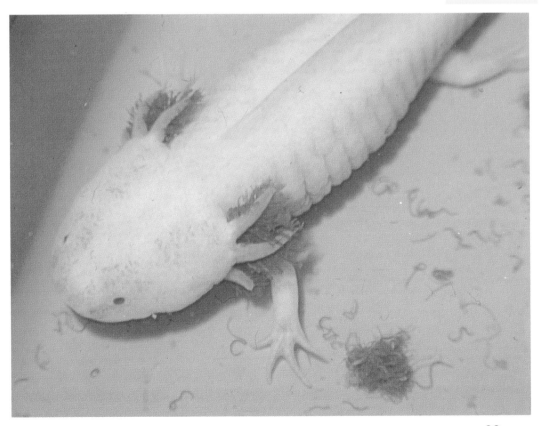

similar in size and shape, although the male may have a slightly broader head and the female a plumper body. When sexually mature, the male will also have a markedly swollen vent region. They may breed from the age of 18 months

axolotls will live 6 to 10 years if given optimum conditions. The male courts the female by making stylized movements with his body. These include bending the body almost double and rapidly wriggling the tail. Eventually he deposits

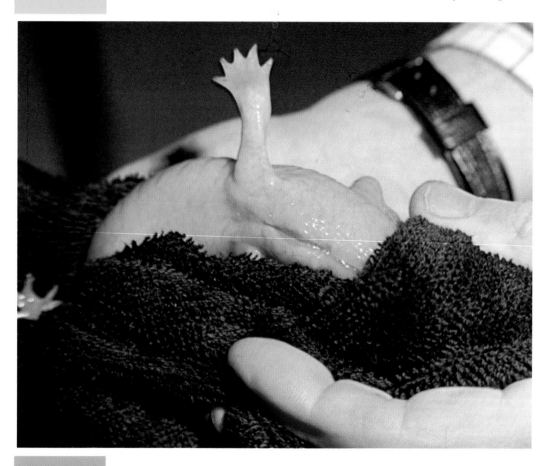

onward, but best results occur when the animals are 30 months old. As the animals age, they become less productive. Most captive

a spermatophore on the substrate close to the female before losing further interest in the proceedings. The receptive female takes the spermatophore into her cloaca, where it will release sperm to fertilize the eggs as they are being laid.

About 48 hours after mating, oviposition will begin. Eggs are laid in batches of 10-30 on the leaves of water plants or on response is required. Then a single pair is housed together in a small tank. A temperature reduction from the normal 17-20°C, down to 10-12°C, usually will result in almost immediate mating behavior, and egglaying can be expected within 48

The female axolotl's cloaca is notably less swollen than the male's. Photo by P. W. Scott.

substrate debris, until altogether 500-800 eggs are laid.

In captivity, it is best to keep sexes separate until a breeding hours. It is best to provide a number of pieces of plastic pipe (12 mm, 0.5 in; electrical conduit is ideal) jammed across the width of the container and

at about half the water's depth, ensuring that you leave plenty of room for the animals to swim between them. Most of the eggs will then be laid on these tubes. After laying, the adults can be returned to their respective stock tanks. The water temperature in the breeding tank can then be slowly raised back to 17-20°C. The water should be fresh, well-aerated, and free of chlorine.

The eggs should hatch within 14 days. Any eggs that turn milky white are infertile and should be removed with a pipette before they decay and pollute the water. On hatching, the tiny axolotls will remain close to the egg case and they will not require food for the first 48 hours as they will still be feeding from the egg sac. After this they may be given infusoria, brine shrimp, and/or water fleas. Pounded lean meat and hard-boiled egg yolk may also be given, but in extremely small quantities to avoid pollution of the water. The larvae soon become active, and at five days of age they should be separated into batches and placed in aerated containers of water about 20 cm (8 in) deep. Well-fed youngsters will grow rapidly, and you will soon be able to give them larger food items such as tubifex, whiteworms, mosquito larvae, and small earthworms. Properly cared for and given a varied diet, young axolotls can reach sexual maturity in as little as six months, but for best results it is advisable to wait until they are nine to twelve months old before this is attempted.

GENERAL BREEDING SCHEMES

Most species of salamander require external stimuli to bring them into breeding condition. Temperate species, for example, usually breed in the spring shortly after hibernation and are affected by increases in temperature, photoperiod, and intensity of light. Tropical species may be influenced by changes in humidity, either seasonal or coincidental. Some species can be persuaded to breed in captivity by injecting them with certain hormones. *Pleurodeles waltl* (the Spanish or ribbed newt) can be induced to spawn by injecting 250 International Units of H.C.G. (human chorionic gonadotrophin), a hormone that is produced by pregnant women. In fact, a certain frog (*Xenopus*) was once used as a pregnancy test for women before more convenient methods were discovered. There is no reason to doubt that certain salamander species could have been used in the same way. Needless to say, if you contemplate using hormone injections to encourage your salamanders to breed, this should be done with the help of a veterinarian or licensed animal technician.

Seasonal breeders that spawn in large bodies of water can be given similar treatment to the axolotl. Water temperature will of course depend on the native habitat of

the species in question. For temperate species, pairs are introduced in the spring, after beginning to gradually increase temperature and photoperiod. These increases should continue until a maximum of 20°C and a 15-hour period of "daylight" have been reached. Amphibious species that live on land after metamorphosis should be given facilities to leave the water as soon as they are ready. This can be done by rearing them in an aquaterrarium with a sloping "bank." Alternatively, they may be reared in shallow water in which large flat stones are placed so that they just break the water surface.

When breeding salamanders that produce great numbers of offspring, it will be necessary to cull some of the larvae in order to prevent overcrowding. As the larvae grow, weed out the smaller specimens and dispose of them—**do not** release exotic specimens that could be a future ecological hazard. It is much better to rear a small number of fit, healthy specimens than to have numerous weaklings.

A Selection of Species

There are about 360 known salamander species, so this little volume does not have room to discuss every species. A number of representative species have been selected for more detailed attention. Further clues to the care of species not covered in detail in this book may be gleaned from a good field guide. Notes on habits, habitat, and distribution will give valuable clues on a strategy for captive husbandry.

In the following discussions the families, for convenience sake, have been placed in alphabetical order. Genera and species have also been listed alphabetically. Lengths given are the maximum to which an

Although not often seen in captivity, the cave salamander, *Eurycea lucifuga*, makes a very good pet. Photo by R. D. Bartlett.

adult specimen of that species may be expected to grow.

FAMILY AMBYSTOMATIDAE

Two genera (*Ambystoma* and *Rhyacosiredon*) and about 30 species, distributed from southern Alaska and Canada to the southern edge of the Mexican Plateau, comprise this family in the restricted sense.

Mexican mountain streams, they probably require very specialized husbandry. In general, members of the genus *Ambystoma* are more suited for the terrarium. A few examples follow.

Ambystoma jeffersonianum Jefferson's salamander

Length: 20 cm (8 in). This is

Dicamptodontidae is very close and formerly was included. The well known axolotl, *Ambystoma mexicanum*, is included in this family; it was covered in detail in the chapter on reproduction. The genus *Rhyacosiredon* has four poorly known species that are unlikely to be available to the terrarium keeper. Living in

a rather plain-looking species but nonetheless makes an interesting terrarium inmate. It is a long, slender species, dark brown to brownish gray above, occasionally with bluish flecks on limbs and lower flanks. It is found in deciduous forests in the northeastern United States, where it usually burrows under surface debris near areas of permanent water. In captivity it requires a cool (15-20°C, 59-68°F) aquaterrarium. It will feed on a variety of small invertebrates. This species is known to hybridize with *A. laterale*, producing all-female offspring.

of North America. Its main habitat is near water in deciduous forest, where it burrows under ground debris. In captivity it should be provided with a small aquaterrarium containing leaf litter. Humidity should be kept high. Summer temperatures of

Ambystoma laterale
Blue-spotted salamander

Length: 12.5 cm (5 in). This is a relatively slender salamander with a narrow snout and short limbs. It is blackish blue above with light blue spots and blotches. The underside is grayish blue with darker blotching. It is found throughout the Great Lakes region and to the Atlantic Coast

15-20°C (59-68°F) are adequate. During the winter, keep at just above freezing (3-4°C, 37-39°F) for two to three months for simulated hibernation. It should be fed on a selection of small invertebrates. Mating occurs in ponds during March and April, and the female lays several batches of 10-15 eggs that are attached to aquatic vegetation

The Blue-spotted Salamander, *Ambystoma laterale.* Photo by R. T. Zappalorti.

The spotted salamander, *Ambystoma maculatum*, is one of the larger species in the family Ambystomatidae, some reaching just under one foot. Photo by K. T. Nemuras.

or debris. Larvae hatch in about 30 days and metamorphose to terrestrial forms in four to six months.

Ambystoma maculatum
Spotted salamander

Length: 25 cm (10 in). One of the larger and more robust species in the family, this salamander has well-developed limbs. Spectacular in color and quite easy to keep, it has become a popular pet species. The ground color is blue-gray and there are two rows of large yellow or orange spots starting on top of the head and extending to the tail tip. The underside is usually a plain slate color. The spotted salamander occurs throughout eastern North America from Nova Scotia and the Great Lakes almost to the Gulf Coast. It is found mainly in areas of

deciduous woodland, rarely far from permanent water. It is an adept burrower and spends most of its time below the surface, but emerges at night or after heavy rains. Captive specimens require a large, woodland type terrarium and will require access to water if breeding is contemplated. The humidity should be kept high. Supplementary heating should not be required; in fact, try and keep the temperature not higher than 25°C (77°F). Feed on various small invertebrates.

Ambystoma opacum
Marbled salamander

Length: 12 cm (5 in). One of the smaller members of the genus, but quite strongly built with well-developed limbs, this species is black with steel-gray marbling. The underside is plain black. It occurs in a variety of woodland sites in the eastern United States from the Great Lakes to the Gulf States, but not the Florida peninsula. Mating occurs on land. The eggs are laid in damp depressions that later fill with

Shown here is an adult marbled salamander, *Ambystoma opacum*, with a newly transformed young. Photo by K. T. Nemuras.

rainwater. The female curls around the ball of eggs and protects it from desiccation until it rains. After hatching, the larvae transform into fully terrestrial forms in four to six months. In captivity it requires maximum size this must be the world's largest land-dwelling salamander species. It is a broad-headed, robust species and makes a fine pet. There are at least six subspecies, exhibiting a huge variation in

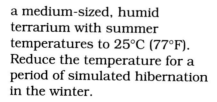

a medium-sized, humid terrarium with summer temperatures to 25°C (77°F). Reduce the temperature for a period of simulated hibernation in the winter.

Ambystoma tigrinum
Tiger salamander

Length: 35 cm (14 in). At its color and pattern. The ground color may be greenish, grayish, or brown with yellow to white spots, stripes, or marbling. It is very widespread across the USA from coast to coast (though often rare and considered endangered in some areas) and extends into Mexico. It occurs in varied habitats

from damp woodland to fairly dry savannah. A secretive, burrowing species, wild tiger salamanders are rarely seen during the daytime unless you are looking for them in deep leaf litter, under and in decaying logs, etc. Courtship and mating take place in temporary pools, lakes, or streams in springtime. The eggs are laid in masses attached to aquatic vegetation. The larvae transform in five to six months. Western populations may be neotenous, retaining their gills and remaining in the water, eventually reaching 35 cm (14 in) in length and reproducing in larval form. Captive specimens require a large aquaterrarium or an aquarium for neotenous specimens. A temperature range of 15-20°C (59-68°F) will suit them fine. Feed on a variety of invertebrates. Hibernate in winter.

FAMILY AMPHIUMIDAE

The amphiumas comprise a single genus containing only three species, making this the smallest salamander family. All three are native to the southern USA and are totally aquatic, having internal gills with the openings just in front of the forelimbs.

Amphiuma means
Two-toed amphiuma

Length: 100 cm (39 in). Probably the best known of the three amphiumas (the other two being *A. pholeter*, the one-toed, and *A. tridactylum*, the three-toed), the two-toed amphiuma is a robust, eel-like salamander with four tiny limbs, each with only two toes.

Although not often kept as pet animals, the amphiumas, like this *Amphiuma pholeter*, make interesting captives and are easily kept in a totally aquatic tank. Photo by R. D. Bartlett.

The lidless eyes are very small and there are no external gills. The color is uniformly dark gray to brown above with a lighter gray underside. It is found in mainly acidic, vegetated, muddy waters including swamps, bayous, and ditches, in the coastal plain of the USA from southeastern Virginia west to Louisiana. It is mainly nocturnal, hiding during the day in submerged burrows. In moist weather conditions it can migrate overland. It feeds on crayfish, frogs, other salamanders, fishes, and even small water snakes.

In captivity it will do well in a large, well-aerated terrarium with a gravel substrate and larger rocks securely arranged to create hiding caves. Aquatic plants will soon be uprooted by the animals, so only floating plants should be used. The water temperature should be maintained at about 24°C (75°F), reduced to 18°C (65°F) in winter for a couple of months. The water must be chlorine-free and unpolluted. Feed on tadpoles, small fishes, pieces of lean meat or heart, or similar items. Crayfishes make a good food if you can get them on a regular basis. Amphiumas mate in the spring. Fertilization is internal. The female seeks out a sheltered depression in the shallows where she lays about 200 eggs and remains coiled about them until they hatch (usually about five months). The larvae are about 5 cm (2 in) long and have external gills like most salamander larvae, but they lose these as they mature. Adults retain a pair of gill slits.

Amphiumas are among the few salamanders than can inflict a painful bite to a human hand. The jaws are strong, and the animal has a habit of twisting wildly when captured, so it is quite capable of drawing blood or even removing some flesh. Caution is advised when handling these salamanders. Many southerners believe (erroneously, of course) that they are venomous. The old name "congo eel" is still often heard.

FAMILY CRYPTOBRANCHIDAE

There are two genera and only three living species in this ancient family. The genus *Andrias* (formerly *Megalobatrachus*) contains two species that are the world's largest salamanders, the giant salamanders of China and Japan, which reach a maximum size of 1.8 and 1.4 m (6 ft and 4ft 8 in), respectively. These giant salamanders are strictly protected as endangered species and as such are unlikely to fall into the hands of the pet keeper

(although they are seen in zoos with some regularity). The genus *Cryptobranchus* contains a single species.

Cryptobranchus alleganiensis Hellbender

Length: 75 cm (30 in). This North American relative of the

Cryptobranchidae is a very old amphibian family which has only two genera. One, *Cryptobranchus*, has only one species, *alleganiensis*, otherwise known as the hellbender, which is represented in these two photographs. Top photo by R. D. Bartlett, bottom by R. T. Zappalorti.

Asian giant salamanders is a large, totally aquatic amphibian with a flattened head and body and a loose flap of skin running along the lower flanks. It has moderately large limbs with four fingers and five toes. There are no external feathery gills, but there is a single pair of gill openings just behind the head. It is grayish brown with darker mottling above, while the underside is lighter and uniform. The male is a little smaller than the female.

Found in the central and eastern United States, the hellbender prefers fast-flowing rivers and streams, especially those with rocky bottoms, where it hides under rocks or in cavities during the day, coming out at night to hunt for food. It feeds on a variety of invertebrates and vertebrates and in captivity will take strips of raw meat or fish. It should be kept only in very large, well-aerated aquaria with a stony substrate and caves for seclusion. Supplementary heating is unnecessary, and the temperature should be reduced in the winter. The animals breed in the late summer to fall, the male excavating a nest cavity beneath large flat rocks or submerged logs. The female lays 200-500 eggs in long strings that are sprayed with milt by the male then pushed together into a tangled mass in

the nest cavity. The male guards the nest until the approximately 2.5-cm (1-in) larvae hatch in two to three months.

FAMILY PLETHODONTIDAE

This is the largest salamander family, containing two subfamilies (Desmognathinae, the dusky salamanders, with three genera; and Plethodontinae, the woodland and bromeliad salamanders with at least 24 genera) with over 220 species. Commonly known as "lungless salamanders" (they breathe through the sensitive moist skin), the plethodontids are primarily found in the New World from southern Alaska and Nova Scotia, through Central America to Brazil and Bolivia; two relict species, however, are found in southern Europe. Many new species have been described in recent years, most of these being from Mexico and Central America.

Although the slimy salamander, *Plethodon glutinosus*, does fairly well in captivity, it cannot be handled much because it secretes a sticky substance that is very difficult to remove from the hands. Photo by R. T. Zappalorti.

Plethodon glutinosus
Slimy salamander

Length: 20 cm (8 in). This is a relatively long, slender species with a round body and a flattened head. It is mainly black with cream or white spots concentrated along the flanks. The underside is slate blue, often mottled with white. It is found over much of the central and eastern USA and into southeastern Canada in a range of habitats from near sea level to 1600 meters (5200 ft),

hiding under rocks and fallen timber and emerging at night. Handle it with care, as its skin secretes a sticky substance that is difficult to remove! It requires a medium-sized, cool terrarium with a gravel and leaf-litter substrate and a few flat stones and plants. Provide a period of simulated hibernation in the winter.

Recent analysis of protein structure and other variation in the slimy salamander has provided evidence that instead

of one species it is a complex of at least 13 similar species with mostly non-overlapping ranges. Similar studies of other woodland salamanders are yielding equally surprising results that are causing many changes in long-established names and species concepts.

Pseudotriton ruber
Red salamander

Length: 18 cm (7 in). One of the most colorful North American salamanders and much prized in the terrarium, there are four subspecies of red salamander ranging in color from bright orange-red to purplish above, with numerous small black spots. The underside is pinkish and may be spotted with black. Found over much of the USA east of the Mississippi River except peninsular Florida, it occurs in very damp habitats, particularly around springs and seepages to altitudes of 1500 meters (4875 ft). It is nocturnal, hiding under cover during the day. It requires a large terrarium with a high humidity. A gravel substrate and mossy rocks will provide the furnishings. Try and provide an artificial drip seepage. The red salamander is typical of a group of plethodontids (comprising over 30 species) where the eggs are laid in shallow water and hatch into aquatic larvae that may

take two years or longer to metamorphose.

FAMILY PROTEIDAE

Comprising two genera and about six species, the Proteidae is often considered the most primitive family of living salamanders. The distribution is unusual and difficult to explain, with *Necturus* (about five species) in the eastern USA and *Proteus* (with a single species) in caves of northeastern Italy and adjacent Yugoslavia. Both genera are completely aquatic, maintaining large gills throughout life and not metamorphosing. The hind feet have only four toes, which distinguishes them from larvae of virtually all other salamanders. This is an assumedly very ancient family. *Proteus anguinus*, the olm of Europe, is almost eel-like, with

Closeup of the head of a mudpuppy, *Necturus maculosus*. Note the attractive stone-like coloration. Photo by Ken Lucas, Steinhart Aquarium.

long, slender limbs and no pigment, adaptations to its completely subterranean existence.

Necturus maculosus
Mudpuppy

Length: 45 cm (18 in). The mudpuppy is the largest and best known of the American proteid salamanders. The aquatic species with four fingers and four toes and a pair of dark red, feathery gills. It is gray-brown to dark gray above with dark-edged bluish gray or brown blotches, while the underside is usually gray with darker markings. Occurring in the central and eastern United States, it may be found in streams, rivers, and lakes. In

mudpuppies and waterdogs (the other four species of the genus) derive their English names from the erroneous belief that they can bark; in fact, their vocal talents are confined to a weakish squeak. The mudpuppy is a robust captivity mudpuppies require a large aquarium with filtered and aerated water at least 30 cm (12 in) deep. The substrate may be medium-grade gravel. The decorations and hiding places can include large stones and tree roots. Feed mudpuppies on small fishes, freshwater shrimps, water snails, and other aquatic animals. Breeding occurs in late spring, when the female lays up to 200 eggs attached beneath rocks, roots, or other debris. These hatch into 2-cm (0.8-in) larvae that may take up to five years to mature.

The other *Necturus* species, the waterdogs, are smaller (seldom exceeding 23 cm, 9 inches) species restricted to southern United States drainages. They inhabit deep leaf litter beds in flowing sandy to gravelly streams and rivers and make nice pets when available.

FAMILY SALAMANDRIDAE

Commonly called the newts, there are 14 genera and some 53 species of typical salamandrids occurring mostly in Eurasia and northern Africa. Only two genera, *Notophthalmus* and *Taricha*, with some six species occur in the New World. Because of increasing protection of the European species due to losses to land development and pollution, several species that once were common in captivity now are seldom seen.

Cynops pyrrhogaster
Japanese fire-bellied newt

Length 10 cm (4 in). This newt is dark chocolate brown above and brilliant, fiery red below. The male's tail becomes bluish or purplish in the nuptial season. It is almost totally aquatic and is found in vegetated ponds only on the Japanese islands of Honshu, Shikoku, and Kyushu. A closely

The Japanese fire-bellied newt, *Cynops pyrrhogaster*, is a very popular pet species that can be kept easily enough in a tank filled with water and a small basking site. Photo by A. van den Nieuwenhuizen.

related species (*C. ensicauda*) occurs on the Ryukyu Islands south of Japan.

In captivity it requires an aquarium with aerated and filtered water to a depth of 20 cm (8 in) and land areas such as mossy rocks or tree roots breaking the surface. Summer temperature should be maintained around 25°C (77°F), but can be reduced to between 5 and 10°C (41-50°F) for a couple of months of simulated hibernation. Feed on small aquatic invertebrates. Breeding occurs in springtime, when courtship and mating take place in water. The eggs are laid on the leaves of aquatic plants such as elodea.

Notophthalmus viridescens
Red-spotted newt

Length: 12 cm (5 in). This newt is very well known in the USA and is noted for the remarkable differences in appearance between the aquatic adults and the juvenile terrestrial form. Adults are smooth-skinned and yellowish to olive-brown above with dark-bordered red spots along each side of the body, sometimes almost forming a line. The underside is yellowish and there are small dark spots all over the body. The terrestrial juveniles, known as red efts, were once thought to be an entirely separate species. These have a rough skin texture and are bright reddish brown to orange all over, with spots of lighter red along the flanks. They are found in eastern North America from southern Canada and the Great lakes region to Florida and eastern Texas. Adults are mainly aquatic, living in shallow

The "red eft" is simply what the red-spotted newt, *Notophthalmus viridescens*, is called during its terrestrial stage. Photo by William B. Allen, Jr.

vegetated waters. In captivity they require a large aquaterrarium that will support both terrestrial and aquatic stages. The temperature should preferably not exceed 22°C (72°F) in summer and should be reduced to around 5°C (41°F) in winter for hibernation. Courtship occurs in water, and 200-400 eggs are laid singly, attached to aquatic vegetation. Gilled larvae hatch in three to eight weeks. These metamorphose into the red efts, which spend one or more years on land before returning to the water as mature adults.

Pleurodeles waltl
Sharp-ribbed newt

Length 30 cm (12 in). This is the largest European salamander, though relatively few specimens actually reach the maximum length of 30 cm (12 in). Heavily built with a broad, flattened head, this is a rough-skinned species with a row of yellow or orange warty tubercles along the flanks through which the sharp tips of the ribs may protrude. The back is olive to grayish yellow with dark brown patches; older specimens are often darker in color. The underside is yellow to off-white or gray, usually with darker blotches. Native to the southwestern two-thirds of the Iberian Peninsula and Morocco, it inhabits water

courses, lakes, ditches, and irrigation systems. It is mainly aquatic unless the water dries up, in which case it estivates until conditions again become favorable. In captivity it requires a planted aquarium with facilities to leave the water (such as a floating platform or

The adult red-spotted newts are very similar in appearance to the young. Photo by Dr. Sherman A. Minton.

55

rocks breaking the surface). Feed on larger invertebrates such as earthworms, freshwater shrimps, crickets, etc. May also take small strips of lean meat. Maintain at 25°C (77°F) (summer) and reduce to around 8°C (46°F) for the winter rest period. Courtship occurs in the water, the male depositing the usual spermatophore that is taken up by the female. Up to 1000 eggs are laid in clumps on water plants or other submersed debris.

Taricha torosa
California newt

Length: 18 cm (7 in). The genus *Taricha* replaces *Notophthalmus* on the western side of North America. The California newt and its close relatives *T. granulosa* (roughskin newt) and *T. rivularis* (redbelly newt) are very similar in general appearance. The California newt is a robust species with a granular skin. It is tan to reddish brown above and orange to yellow below. When breeding, the male's skin becomes smooth and his tail becomes compressed. When alarmed or attacked by predators, this newt arches its body to expose the bright underside. Found in coastal California and the California Sierras, where it inhabits evergreen and oak forests near permanent water, it is terrestrial except during the breeding season. Captive

specimens should be provided with a large aquaterrarium with a planted land area. Keep at 22°C (72°F) during the summer and reduce to around 10°C (50°F) for a couple of months in winter. Feed on a variety of small invertebrates. The California newt breeds in water from December to May and lays its eggs on aquatic plants. Larvae may metamorphose during the first season or during the following spring.

Salamandra salamandra
Fire salamander

Length: 28 cm (11 in). The salamander of the ancients and subject of much folklore, the European fire salamander is a handsome fellow with a livery of bright yellow or orange on a glossy black background. The yellow markings may be arranged in spots, blotches, or stripes, depending on geographical variation. There are many subspecies. It occurs in western, central, and southern Europe, northwestern Africa, and parts of southwestern Asia. It mainly inhabits heavily forested areas, usually in hilly or mountainous country. It lives in damp conditions, rarely far from water, and hides under ground litter during the day, coming out at night to hunt for food. In captivity it should be provided with a large unheated aquaterrarium with moving (aerated) water. It should be provided with adequate refuges such as flat stones, hollow branches, etc. Feed on a variety of invertebrates. Hibernate in winter at lower temperatures. Courtship and mating occur on land. The female deposits developed larvae into suitable waters.

Triturus marmoratus
Marbled newt

Length: 16 cm (6.3 in). The genus *Triturus* contains 12 species of typical European newts. *T. marmoratus* is a colorful species, being marbled with green, brown, and black with a yellow vertebral stripe. The underside is gray to whitish with darker mottling. During the breeding season, the male develops a prominent untoothed dorsal crest. Its natural range is southwestern France and the Iberian Peninsula, where it replaces *T. cristatus*. Where the ranges of the two species overlap,

hybrids of great beauty may occur. *T. marmoratus* spends most of the year on land, often in relatively dry situations. In captivity it should have a large aquaterrarium maintained at 20-25°C (68-77°F), with a reduction to around 10°C (50°F) for simulated hibernation. Feed on a variety of small invertebrates. Breeds in the water in the earlier part of the year.

Triturus vittatus
Banded newt

Length: 15 cm (6 in). In its breeding dress the male banded newt must be the most spectacular of all newts, especially the subspecies *T. v. ophryticus*. The ground color is reddish brown covered with small dark spots. A broad, black-bordered, silvery white stripe extends along the flanks between the limbs. The underside is yellow to orange. The body crest of the breeding male is deeply serrated and as much as twice the depth of the body. The broad, flattened tail is also crested on both edges and is marked with blue and green blotches. This species occurs in Asia Minor and

Marbled newts, *Triturus marmoratus*, are known for spending much of their time in dry, sometimes very warm, surroundings, which is somewhat unusual for most salamanders and newts. Photo by J. K. Langhammer.

adjacent Russia through southeastern Turkey to northern Iraq, Syria, Lebanon, and Israel. It usually occurs in damp areas above 1000 meters (3250 ft). Give it a medium aquaterrarium with temperatures to 25°C (77°F) in summer reduced in winter for hibernation. Feed on a variety of small invertebrates.

Triturus vulgaris
European common or smooth newt

Length: 10 cm (4 in). Outside the breeding season, this little newt is a fairly drab brownish in coloration. In full breeding dress, however, the male takes on breathtaking beauty. He develops a high, continuous wavy crest, large dark blotches develop on the body, a bluish flash develops along the lower margin of the tail, and the orange color of the belly intensifies. The female is usually olive brown with a less intense belly color and smaller black spots. This is an abundant species in much of Europe and into Asia, though it is absent from Iberia, being replaced there by *T. boscai*. Mainly terrestrial, it spends the day under ground litter in damp situations, rarely far from permanent water. Provide a medium-sized aquaterrarium with adequate hiding places on land. Like other European newts, it breeds in spring after entering water.

Hygiene and Health

The importance of hygiene to animals confined in a relatively small space such as the terrarium cannot be underestimated. By hygiene we are not necessarily talking about soap and disinfectants, but in its most general sense mean prevention of disease. Of course, cleanliness is a very important aspect of hygiene, but so is providing your terrarium inmates with optimum conditions for a contented life devoid of stress. Stress in itself can be a factor that reduces an animal's normal resistance to disease, so we must ensure that our salamanders' housing is as comfortable as possible for them.

Salamanders and newts generally are not very adaptable to surroundings that are alien to them. Just imagine what happens when you remove a salamander from cool, peaty, moist woodland and place it in a terrarium containing chlorinated tap water at room temperature in your house and leave the lights on until midnight. Common sense will tell you that this is just the thing to cause stress. As discussed earlier, light intensity, photoperiod, and temperature should be similar to that found in the amphibian's native habitat. Excessive chlorine, copper, hardness, or acidity in various domestic water supplies can be dangerous to an amphibian's health. Having a very sensitive and permeable skin can mean lethal amounts of chemicals

Some of the more delicate caudates, like this smallmouth salamander, *Ambystoma texanum*, from Michigan, are particularly sensitive to unclean surroundings. Photo by R. T. Zappalorti.

being taken up before you realize what is happening. Use pond or river water whenever possible. Because of increased contaminants and excessive acidity of rainwater over some of the globe, you can no longer be sure that even fresh rainwater will be suitable. If you have no alternative but to use tap water, allow it to stand for at least 24 hours to allow free chlorine to disperse before it is used. If you have sudden or inexplicable deaths among your salamanders, it may be worth having the water chemically analyzed.

HANDLING

Remember that many salamanders and newts have powerful protective poisons that they release from glands in the skin. Some of these can be extremely dangerous if you get them in your eyes or mucous membranes. Therefore, always wash hands thoroughly after handling amphibians. Some

species are also unable to tolerate the poisons of others, so don't keep more than one species in a cage unless you are absolutely sure they are tolerant of each other.

DISEASES AND TREATMENTS

When kept in optimum environmental conditions and with good hygienic practices, amphibians are remarkably resistant to diseases. Most cases of ill health can usually be blamed on some inadequacy in the care. Some of the more common afflictions include the following:

Nutritional Deficiencies

Caused usually by a lack of certain minerals or vitamins in the diet, deficiencies are likely to occur among salamanders fed on a monotonous diet of things like mealworms. It is important to provide your animals with as great a variety of foodstuffs as possible. A routine application of a powdered multivitamin and mineral supplement to the food will prevent such deficiencies.

Redleg Disease

This is the most infamous disease of captive amphibians and is caused by the bacterium *Aeromonas hydrophila*. Symptoms include reddening of the skin, especially on the belly

and the undersides of the limbs. Infected animals become lethargic and apathetic and should should be immediately isolated. If caught in its early stages, redleg may be treated by immersing the infected animal for about 15 seconds in a 2% solution of copper sulfate or potassium permanganate. The use of an antibiotic such as tetracycline may also help. Consult a veterinarian for advice about this lethal disease. Treatment with copper and permanganate solutions may be almost as dangerous as the disease itself. Because redleg is a stress disease, never overcrowd salamanders and be sure that the cage is always spotless.

Fungal Infections

Saprolegnia and other fungi can be troublesome in aquatic amphibians and in larvae. The disease is seen as areas of inflamed skin surrounded by whitish tissue. Untreated, these infections can prove fatal. If caught in its early stages, a fungus infection can be treated by immersing the animal in a 2% solution of malachite green or Mercurochrome for five minutes, repeating after 24 hours if symptoms do not improve. Larvae should be treated by keeping them in a solution of 0.001% chloramine (paratoluol sodium sulfonchloramide) for 24 hours, then in fresh water for three days; repeat the initial treatment.

To keep your salamanders and newts as healthy looking as this mole salamander, *Ambystoma talpoideum*, you have to accept the fact that a lot of patience, time, and attention will be required. Photo by R. D. Bartlett.

INDEX

Page numbers in **boldface** refer to illustrations.

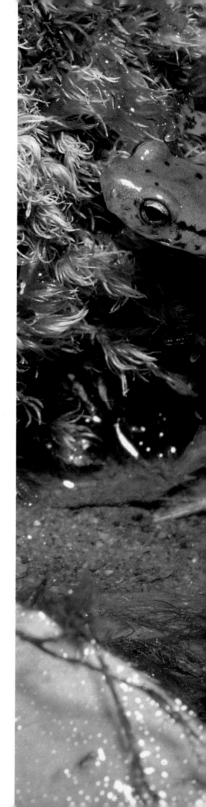